The Phoenix
& The Fireflies

Sutrishna Sen

BookLeaf
Publishing

India | USA | UK

Presentation by *BookLeaf Publishing*

Web: www.bookleafpub.com

E-mail: info@bookleafpub.com

ISBN: 9789363310209

First edition 2024

ACKNOWLEDGEMENT

Nothing worthwhile in the world happens without the help of a few good friends. So, I would extend my sincerest gratitude to those friends who managed to keep their trust in me and made me continue writing, and friends who shared their genuine suggestions on my write-ups, on and off social media. Their presence and contributions are truly magical. If I know even a little bit about selfless love, then these humans with no blood relations are the sole reasons for that. Thank you for being my friend.

I am deeply grateful for the support of my mother and elder sister in my decisions. Also, the trust my late father had in my creative expressions will always be a proud and blessed memory for me.

Then, there are people whom we meet for some countable moments in our journey, but we can still count on them. To all such people in my life, whom I cannot address with a single word, thank you for filling my life with your much-needed occasional acts of love. I am honoured to receive your encouragement.

Lastly, I am grateful for the opportunity provided by Book Leaf Publishing. Thank you for organising this contest and keeping us motivated to write a book. Their endeavour has successfully diminished the gap between dreaming and doing.

Preface of the Book
By the Book

*T*hey said, "Life is short"!

"*H*ey, I'm alike," said this book,

"*E*nvision the things you've never consciously
thought about"

"*P*icture the emotions as you read,

*H*aving your favourite beverage by your side.

*O*bserve the thoughts changing their shades,

*E*nchanted in the forest of feelings.

*N*otice how your heart travels

*I*n the spaces between these words.

*X*anadu, you may call, but only when you've
reached there."

&

"*T*hen, as you are lost in these pages,

*H*ope, you feel found in parallel,

*E*mbracing the magic of this contrasting fusion.

*F*eel heard by these untuned songs in the wind;

*I*n your usual silence, feel understood.

*R*elive those emotions in your veins,

*E*liminated once in the name of adulthood.

*F*rame these memories without photographs,

*L*et your senses cast some sweet spells.

*I*mbibe the power of rebirth and light,

*E*xpressed as the phoenix and the fireflies;

*S*hare your gifts with the ones in need,

shun the ones who come otherwise."

TABLE OF CONTENTS

Grooves of Gravity

Weekdays' Wind

I cherish coming back to the wind,
On the working days of the week.
The moment I step on my lane,
She comes rushing like that person,
Who shares an unmatched affection, but
Whose presence gets overlooked, often.
She comes with all her enticements, but
I approach with an air of enfeeblement.
We meet briefly to say goodbye,
With an assurance of meeting later,
Not known, when.

I enter my home,
With the upcoming tasks running
through my head.
While pulling the curtains aside
I see her dashing
Across the ground and around the trees,
From the tip of small grasses
to the top of the giant greens.
As if, asking everyone about their day
Before the sun goes down,
For another night.

We meet again the next evening,
She never forgets to greet me,
Hardly cares if our meeting is momentary!

I rejoice at her adorable dedication,
She rejoices in my daily homecoming.

Weekly Silence

On weekends,
We meet again.
When my mind is no longer a camp of
self-imposed urgencies,
I take out time for her, or
Maybe, she takes me out of my so-called
important self.
We talk, if not for hours,
Then for one hour, for sure.

She meets me with her everyday excitements.
From my right, she pulls my little black hair, and
Whispers a 'whoosh' in my left ear.

She talks about all the stories she has gathered
On her ritualistic evening get-togethers
With the grasses, with the flowers,
with the leaves, and with the clouds.
I keep listening to her, open-mouthed.
She dries up all the moisture of pain on my skin,
And I don't know how she does the same
With my heart, with my soul, and with my mind.
She never attempts anything extraordinary to
please me.
She just is herself, and
I find a new self of mine
Every weekend we meet,
Every time we talk this way.
Needless to say, that
I look forward to this ceremonial silence.

Bird Home

On some days, I wish
Birds could also have
ownership of properties.
The properties they choose to dwell in,
The shrubs, the plants, or the giant trees.
Ownership, as humans have, but
Unlike concrete buildings.
I wish they could have an entitlement
To own spaces, as much as they have the
Freedom to abandon them and
find a new settlement.

I wish humans would ask for their consent
Before uprooting their homes, so deliberately.
As if, they had chosen to settle illegally.
I don't know the language of birds, but
The language of humans should try

Respecting their spaces
and not just human houses.
I don't know about their laws, but
The laws of humans should try
Accepting their territories,
Unmarked and uninjured.

Because unlike human homes
Which remain abandoned, sometimes,
The homes in nature
continue to serve their purpose
Diligently, irrespective of being taken care of.

Evolutionary Ego

How unaware I was that,
The passionate compulsion to announce
Supremacy over others wasn't just a matter of
Community, culture, language, or religion.
There has been one big lie,
Propagated since
The beginning of human evolution!
You'd be more than delighted to have known,
That lie does not discriminate
humans against each other,
On any ground.
But I found it disappointing to discover,
That lie just feeds our collective human ego!
So, even if for one miracle of a minute

We forget all self-created boundaries,
We're united by an imaginary theory that
Humans are better
than all other beings of living!
Just because we speak and we have a medium?
Just because we form societies and
live in conjunction?
Just because we left the wild, formed cities, and
marked boundaries?
Does that make us supreme as living beings?
Did we ever learn to stop all the fights
by merely speaking?
Then how did we become so outstanding?
When all other species kept communicating but
It's just now that we are discovering!
When all other beings realise
their invisible boundaries,
We sign intellectual papers and still break into
each other's territories!
Though we left the wilds long ago,
We could never stop feeding our false ego-
"We are better than them!"

The constant urge to compare;
The barren desire to feel better.
Is that how the intelligent mind works?
I wonder,
Or are we mentally still in a mode of survival?

We try to ensure our
Safety by claiming to be the strongest,
Continuity by claiming to be the smartest, and
Resourcefulness by mislabeling
our greed as a requirement.
So that our lives are not in danger,
So that we have enough evolutionary answers,
So that we always have a reason for our hunger!
Tell me,
Why do we still believe that we are better?

Only if we could understand this
unsaid rule of the wild, that
Competitions and comparisons are
Indubitably not the key to a better life;
That the giraffe never tries to be like the deer;
That the differences need not rule out each other.

The wild lives without commitments,
without boundaries so clear.
After having all of that,
why do we still need to fear?
We covered up our incompetencies,
saying they are inferior!
While they've been religiously busy
with their purpose,
We need to awaken ourselves
in this self-created human chaos.
We look at Mother Nature,

Draw all our inspirations from Her.
We jump with our names in the air,
When the connections between the dots
become clearer.
Oh, this fallacy of being superior,
Is ego's easiest escape from a delusive danger!

Palette on Pupils

As I let my eyes scroll,
Over the vast stretches of greens,
I also see a few towers in between.
Grey clouds full of rainy hopes,
Try to tease their metallic heads.
But by some invisible giant ropes,
They are slowly pulled aside.

On another side of this cluttered sky,
I see cottony white clouds,
As blank as my next page.

With no colours of anticipation and
Yet to be scratched about.

Somehow, these two meet in the giant field
I have been watching;
To blend and lose all memories.
All the memories of colours and hope,
Carried so childishly, so far around.
"Where is the white? Where is the grey?
Where are the hopes of rain?"
ask the bright sun rays.

From the window, as I watch all this,
A palette of prominence forms on my pupils;
The green at the bottom, followed by the white,
And the big greyish lid of hope on the top
Until they decide to mix and lose it all.
All the while I smile and think,
How so wonderful are temporary things.

A Lot to Talk

The photos in my gallery
Of the natural sunrise,
Over the small cliff;
Of the vibrant kingfisher,
In the early morning;
Of the bright purple flower,
Fallen peacefully on the street,
Of the reflecting raindrops,
On the fresh green leaves;
Speak of something,
I've not been quite understanding.
Other than the things
We think they say about—
A new day, a new hope;
Even the beautiful needs to work out;
Life is ultimately lost, no matter how beloved;
A growing plant needs water to reach its roots.
I assume they've said this enough,
Hardly bothering, if we ever heard.

Yet, every day,
there's this thought that sprouts—
They've still got to say a lot.
If not a lot, then at least
Something subtle yet powerful!

I keep photos like these in my gallery,
Thousands of those, believe me.
I assume, one day,
I might figure their riddles out.
Why do ordinary things look so profound
Day in and day out?

I wonder if they wish to say that,
"Do not try to listen to us.
Have you ever seen us doing that?"
As if they again smirked,
How rarely they need us
To go about their gifted days on earth.
They continued sharing
Those indecipherable words,
"In your assumptions, do not try to amuse us.
Do we ever try to do so?
Do not try to find your clues in us,
Questions of which you have cleverly set up,
Answers to which you have already drawn up.
Look into yourself as much as you look at us.
There is a mirror kept undisturbed,
Waiting for its only master.

You roam around to see your reflection,
Almost overlooking,
The easiest place for it to be found.
See right there.
Pause, if you need to.
Capture that moment in your memory and
With those, try adding colours to your gallery.
As vibrant as the kingfisher,
As natural as the cliff,
As bright as the purple flower,
As fresh as the rain-soaked greens."
Oh! look, how I did what they asked me not to,
Or is it the reflection of me,
talking in their names?

Powerfully Planted

The new leaves of the sapling
are busy enjoying
their first meeting with the wind,
gentle and caressing.
Do they feel the fear of being torn
when the wind grows strong?
They have no one to protect them from
the gusty blows.
How alone!
How brave and beautiful!
They are on their own!

The wind grows.
The two leaves start flapping more.
Are they still enjoying it?
Or is it the vibration of fear crawling in?
Do they understand what that is?
Fear? Of loss, of death, of calamities?
Or are these just ways
to keep human havoc in line?
I don't know, but I hope they don't.

If they had,
They'd have died a thousand deaths
in their entire lifetime.
Do they feel like giving up
even before they are forcibly made to bend?
I think humans only look for
human emotions in everything non-human!
Maybe Mother Nature planted Her bravest ones
on the ground, and
Asked others to build a home,
sweet, safe, and sound!

Signs of Seasons

The falling of leaves,
The blooming of flowers,
The withering of branches,
The drooping of buds.
Nature is mysteriously so expressive at times,
When the changing shadows indicate
How the seasons are winding.
I wish we could also come with
Such evident signs on our appearance,
So we didn't have to spend countless seasons
Hoping the shadows would someday turn bright!
Imagining the buds would regain their strength
to stay upright,
Wishing the branches would reverse
the signs of ageing, and
Praying the leaves will maintain their green
At least till the flowers become receptive.

I wish we could also come with such signs,
To plan our life in and around it,
Just like our vacations in summer or
winter times.

Breathless Blooms

An ineffable affair about nature
Goes mostly unnoticed
In the absence of an observer;
The matter that makes
The elements of Mother Earth,
Unexplainably incomparable
to their human counterparts.
The thing about the lifetime of the living,
Of the human body, of the little buds,
Of the dance of the Black Drongos,
Of the Bulbul's indecipherable words.
Our big humaneness feels

Human life is bigger than all of these,
Stays longer than these subtle characteristics.
I had been of that opinion too,
Until my educated ego was broken beautifully.
Seven years passed since his last sigh,
Eight years since he stayed up all night,
Lost in the sweet-soothing memories
Is the time he last smiled.
Yes, I try rewinding those, but
The inevitability sits heavy on my eyes.
I stand on the balcony;
Teary eyes sweep over the garden.
There are these big yellow flowers
Which bloomed in bunches, after Dad died, and
Continued to bloom years after his demise!
As if, keeping some secret promises to the one
Whose hands have them carefully planted,
Whose eyes would've danced
Calling this usual as enchanted.
*I realised that love is not a one-time act with
Mother Nature.*
The branches continue blooming,
even if the person
Planting them stops breathing forever,
*Irrespective of the plants being of nourishment
or disaster!*

Moves around Unmovable

How do these leaves feel
With every touch of the pouring rain?
How happily they get drenched!
Don't they? You must have seen it.
With no childish attempts of holding
Those drops, which touch their body,
Bringing them to life, and in no time,
Sliding to the other, and dropping just below.

How do these branches feel,
When the ants climb up and down
Their slender spines?
How effortlessly they allow
To walk, run, or move all over them!
With no intention of calculating
How much they provide and
How little they receive, in return.

How do these flowers feel,
When they finally open up their petals and
See the beautiful butterflies coming?
With no doubt if
They would be worthy enough
To receive the pollinator's kiss!

The leaves don't chase the sun,
Nor do they blame the rain.
The branches never feel the need to put a
"No Trespassing" board on them.
The flowers never have to run after the bees
to announce they are open,
Yes, the trees can't move themselves,
yet make so many things move around them.

Prayer for Prosperity

I pray that
You become rich.

Rich enough to
See a big sky,
Full of clouds of diverse colours,
forms, and mischiefs,
Watch the birds in a flock
Flying back home
At the end of the day
In a unique pattern,
That makes you believe

You are in alignment with the universe;
Notice the trees in your garden,
Trying to tease you
With an obstructed view
Of the gorgeous evening sky.
But you still love the usual scattered rainbow
around yourself,
Having colours, you don't know how to christen.

I hope you see
The windows of the adjacent apartment lit up
Unbothered to follow
any pre-planned pattern, and
It hits you softly that
Everyone has their timelines in a day, in a life.

I hope you can listen, when
The crickets start to announce their presence.
The air around you makes you crave
A comforting warmth,
The insects oscillate near the street lights,
While the sound of the vehicle horns
becomes fainter.

I hope, you become rich enough
To feel this symphony.
I hope you become powerful enough
To know where the real power lies.

And by the time you become aware that
You are smiling with some invisible joy,
I hope you know that
You were never lost,
You were just present
In this "what's next?" world.

Midnight Mousse

I watch the city lights gleaming,
The vehicles that don't stop speeding,
Amidst the darkness which might be sleeping.
I quench my midnight craving for a mousse—
Am I living in a poem? I am amused.
I wish to witness the best this morning.
It's 5:10 and I feel as fresh as
the soon-to-come first rays of sunshine.
There appears a shade of orange
Marking the long lines of the sky,
Only one solo star blinks like me, I find.
As some of the orange layers
begin transmuting into yellow,
The midnight shade just above

also starts turning azure.
As I capture this coloured canvas with my phone
and my mind,
The mauve makes
a magnificent match meanwhile.
Then, I watch the sun squeezing its eyes
After another night of slumber at those
untouched heights.
The wind nudges the clouds reminding
Another morning's arrival to these lazy fluffies,
But where are the birds?
Haven't heard them sing so far!
Next, I let myself gaze upon
the rivers flowing down.
I look at my watch to count,
how many more minutes to swallow
This sky, now a monochrome, and
being cuddled by the cottony scouts.
It's 6:10 now, as I look outside the window.
"People on the right who were awake have
witnessed the winter line,
I hope," the pilot just announced.
"Yes, I did," I'd have screamed. Though
It's a failed attempt to capture it in words,
you know.
Not from a hill-top, or a mountain peak, but
*With a midnight mousse
in the middle of the clouds!*

Conflicts in Compassion

Immortal Instincts

Expecting eternal love,
From an exscinding life,
Is like trying to find the end of the sea
Which seems possible sometimes!
For life is lived to die, and
Our desires are feeble.
Determinations can conquer, but
We also dream of things unworkable!
For life always demands logic, they say,
Where fairy tales find no place!
Dreams that amuse us at night,
Are burnt in the first sun rays.
The body decays during demise,
Spreading our emotions in the air.
If death engulfs everything,
Are the feelings spared?

If life is transient, indeed,
How can instincts carry a fragment of forever?
How can we 'just know' things,
We never really knew earlier?

Pasture of Prayers

Far, far away,
Where our prayers sway;
Like unwoven threads in the air,
They fly and wish to fly away.
With the soft blowing breeze,
Their wings unfreeze;
Like an eagle in the sky,
Their flight refuses to cease.
Unlike a larva in the deep blue ocean,
Lost somehow, doesn't know home lane,
Is taken away by water currents;
These prayers know,
Where they need to go.
These prayers swing,
Try to reach the King.
The King of all pain, the King of all blessings—

God, the Almighty, the Shepherd of Prayers.
Turns some true, and saves some for later.
Then, the former comes back to earth,
As if gravity is their friend on this journey, and
It does not play with their path.
The prayers reach their possessors
Whose life then finds a new verse.

When wishes return as Divine Bliss,
The strength of the invisible love grows stronger.

Failure to Feel

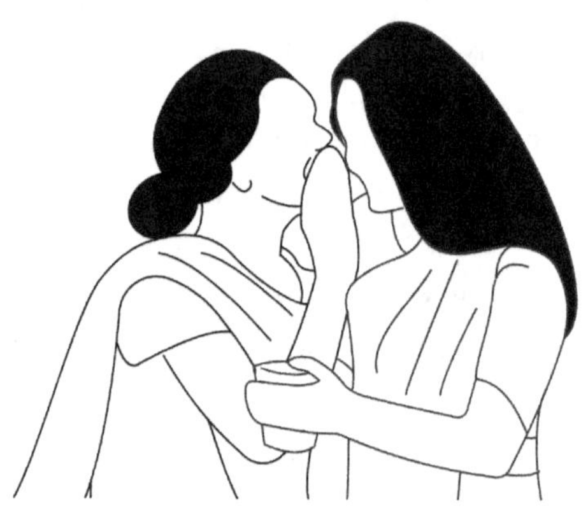

So many compositions,
Lots of anticipation,
Finite feelings, infinite on their own.
Ever wonder who decides
Which one would receive the most recognition?
Whose happiness is it
that feels like a dream for all?
Whose pain might shake the whole world?
I am wandering in the emotional hall,
Trying to find the answering scroll.
Nurtured by the human society and also blamed,
Words hardly find any place here for them.
"If you follow your instincts,
You might get all you think"
Said the old lady,
noting my expression so blank.

Loving someone like a baby,
Or disrelishing someone like an enemy!
Such comparisons with emotions,
Is it so necessary?

When someone is reluctant to feel,
No words in the Universe can borrow it at will.
When our beloveds can empathise with
our unsaid feelings,
That happiness is what,
one might dream of enjoying.
When even our words fail to convey,
What we want the world to feel for us,

The pain of having those letters
lingering on your lips,
Might shake up your entire world.

Grudgeless Giggles

Amidst the inevitability of growing old,
In your roguish, magnetic recollections,
I hope you still live those afternoons,
When you did not choose
to comfortably drowse.
You still talk about those television soaps,
To which your heart and mind
always chose to devote.
You still remember the rules
you intentionally broke,
As proud achievements,
now you love to share those.
From the taste of an old candy,
the smell of the first rain,
The sound of your father coming home, and
To the sight of your then-best friend;
I hope you feel joy at the thoughts of
your attuned attention back then, and

How you collected all the happiness hues,
always!

To this date,
When you are busy becoming a person,
You are yet to be,
And the crowd of uncertainties
clouds your mind,
I hope you have a colourful childhood to rewind.
When the discomfort of sleeplessness
weakens your body,
I hope the comfort of sweet memories
becomes your remedy.
When the characters in your waking life
confuse your heart,
I hope the fictional stories from the past
restore your trust in love.

So, I also wish that
children could have a childhood
Full of mistakes, mischiefs, giggles, and
some good memories of making many friends,
The relief of not knowing resentment, and
Moments that feel like
centuries of being truly alive!
I pray we can create a world
Where our children can witness
a sky free of missiles;
Where they can roam around,

Without knowing the burden of being bound.
Because we can show them that
Being boundless and being unsafe
are not the same.
I hope we can let our children express,
What their minds and hearts are passionate
about,
Because they are rational enough to learn that
Self-expression is not an excuse for disdain.

I hope we can let them play in the
neighbourhood,
With kids who speak different tongues,
Who come from different cultures and
enjoy varied foods,
Be it subtle or not,
Because we can assure them that,
A genuine friendship does not need
only similarities to bloom.

I hope they can see the peacock dance and
Not just read about it in their school textbooks.
Witness the journey of trees from a small seed
And not just know the science
behind earthly life.
I imagine them getting drenched in the rain,
Playing outdoor games with another five,
if not ten.
I hear their grudgeless giggles after a big fight.

And see them come running home together
When the sun is no longer in sight.
I sense their hunger that knows no worries;
It believes it will be quenched
once they reach home.
I believe we don't need to be the Creator
To create such a time
When their eyes can see sweet dreams and not
nightmares of landmines!

Devil's Blessings

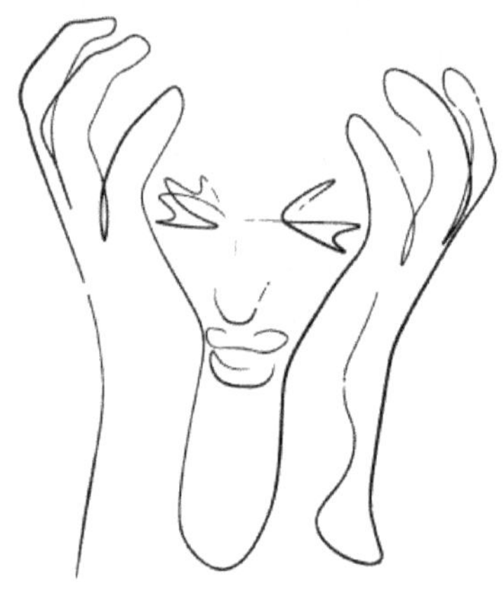

Amidst an almost calm surrounding,
Came these words flying,
Which I couldn't avoid:
"She is not like them,
She doesn't talk much in person, and
When she does, on rare occasions,
Just notice her pronunciation.
I've read her writings,
But why is she reluctant to engage in
conversation?
Is it because she is hesitant?"
Listening to all this, replied the other person,
"She might be hesitant, but
She might also be trying.
She might not wish to do it like others, but

She'd find out her style ."
"Why can't she just try to be like others,
When others are already better than her?
She can follow their styles.
After all, it isn't that bad, is it?"
"But I'd love for her to discover her own.
When she is already not like them,
Why should she try to fit in?
Is her individuality so unacceptable?"
"Wouldn't it take so much time?
Wouldn't she be too late?
What if her style is not liked?
Wouldn't her efforts go in vain?
Why should she work the hard way?
When following someone else is easier?"
It seemed to go on forever.
Their conversation was making me feel weaker.
I tried to run away from there, but
Every place I went, the voices got louder.
I looked at the people around me,
They seemed to be playing the same symphony.
Agitated, I just closed my eyes, and
To my surprise, I could hear it more clearly.
How do you turn something unheard?
How can you silence the echo of the words?
No, we cannot do that. God had been clever.
He wanted us to mind our guard.
I thought to myself,
I might have been to the wrong place.

But when I stopped listening to
the noise outside,
I realised,
The devil inside me was arguing with my angel.
I see no way to escape from this.
I can only choose what I speak.
Or, if I still fail at that,
I might just learn to stay indifferent to it.

The voices, the nightmares,
the devil, and the fears,
Might continue to live inside me forever.
They might try to make me listen to their
powers,
But also the peace, the dreams,
the angels, and the valour!
I know if I just choose
Which ones to pay attention to,
*Even the devil would learn
to make peace with me,
Even the voices would learn
to speak of my valour!*

Unsung Poetry

Of course, you are right,
"Nobody reads poetry.
Why should they?
Why would anyone?"

Of course, it has changed.
Words no longer rhyme.
"All good has been written.
What better could you still find?
It's the same pain and the same perspectives;
Same metaphors and superlatives.
You see, everyone is writing.
These days, poetry has lost its objectives."

I see, you are self-assured,
In your dismissal of poetry's worth.
Yet the songs you come back to,
Still, speak of their artistry.
Some music, some beats,
Intense efforts to make that touching treat!

You claim poetry is dying,
While your playlist still has the flavours of
poesy.

Of course, you are right,
You no longer read poems at night,
But here's a missing piece,
Let me bring it to light,
You are just reading the words here;
Yet to be played, are the hymn and the highs!

Uncomfortable Privilege

People often remark,
As they do these days,
"Everyone is doing it.
There isn't anything singular."

But that's what's special, isn't it?
That everyone gets to do it?
Remember,
our parents have said this for years,
"We can't do it like them,
We aren't privileged enough!"

Now that we are,
We are surprisingly uncomfortable!
Maybe because after decades of
Seeing and believing,
Why you cannot do,
What you aspire to,
It is really difficult,
To see so many already living their dreams!

We've been used to only
Rare legendary stories and
Some countable success glories.
But now that everyone is dreaming and
achieving,
That too, fairly decently,
We're not ready to witness.
At least not so presently.
Maybe that's why it is distressing,
How the excuses of not dreaming are fading!
Or, you can say,
The reasons for not doing the same.

We've never understood each other so well.
We've only counted minutes while interacting.
Now that the world has become boundless,
We sense
The interest in conversations is increasing.
While there are people
Who still won't love those endless talks,

Others consider it a privilege.
While there are people,
Who'd still love to be cosy in their blankets or
Spend time with their babies.
There are also those
Who would watch a new movie, or
Pick up a new book of poetry.

The pattern has been like this
since the beginning:
The world presents itself in its own ways,
Irrespective of whether we
choose to accept or deny.
All we can do is get used to it.

Villain's Lies

Sometimes people push you away
With the burdens of mistakes,
you never made.
So that they can live peacefully with
the lies that they were told.
The lies that they love to
tell themselves each night.
We find peace in believing
The truth can be blamed for pain,
Forever;
Not realising the same lies in hindsight
Turn us into the bigger villain
Sooner or later!

Vocab of Emotions

The day I came to this realisation,
I was freed from
the chains of unintended misinterpretations.
We don't understand words
by their set definitions
Or meanings
which they are supposed to convey in particular.
Instead, we understand them the way
We have associated them in our memories.

Mom is a wonderful, unbiased word in general.
When I say 'mom,'
the love of your mother might fill your heart
Yet the same word might bring tears to
someone's eyes,

Whose mom has embraced death,
while bringing the one to life.
Words are not
what they mean in the dictionaries,
They change their context
based on a person's emotional vocabulary.

Listen to Solve

I primarily read non-fiction and
try to write poetry.
You will find me preaching, teaching,
motivating
Like it's my second nature and
I know you might be tired of it all!
But I can also jump into the river of sadness
Continue to go with the flow,
With a million others crying beside me,
With no changes or solutions
to my pain or theirs.

So, I might walk with you
a few steps in your pain,
But eventually, I will ask you to come out.
I will tell you how things can be changed.
I will urge you to try,
I will encourage you to fight.
I know the acts of listeners
are justifiably overrated.
But that overshadows the value
These people provide.
These people can help you see
The picture beyond
the confines of your sorrow.
The people who can present a bird's eye view
Of all that remains unseen,
That is what would help you go on,
my dear friend.

I know, having someone listening might help
for the time being.
But won't you let your tears dry and
*Try walking on the path of solution
before it's too late?*

Texting Silence

I had been sending long texts full of
Depths and desires,
Dreams and devastations,
Screams and smiles,
Regrets and realisations,
To people full of themselves,
Who don't care for the intentions of the words,
Just use them to brag about their worth.
Who don't know how to read emotions,
Just use them to prove
Their greatness as humans.
Who are unwilling to understand
what's conveyed,
And use silence
as the only mode of communication.

I used to foolishly send long texts
to these people,
Who never read but
willfully misinterpreted my words.
I witnessed
passionate words becoming poisonous
in their presence,
I watched heartfelt communications becoming
conflicts
With their consent, so generous, and
I had cried wondering where I had gone wrong.
I questioned, doubted, and
blamed my own words.
Only to realise,
What had never been the true trouble,
Could never provide a real resolution.

So, I changed the ways I express myself, and
Grabbed a pile of hopeful blank papers.
I sent those heaps of hopeless, habitual letters,
Saw them evolve into poems, filling pages, and
Becoming books that people do not try to alter.

Actionable Words

Of all the guidance and tips,
The realisations and clicks,
So much said about the dos and don'ts,
Advice consumed but actions followed zeroes,
There is one thing, about human relationships
That spoke to me through the least possible
letters and
It is best put this way:
Witness words but
Accept actions.

Because some well-educated people can be seen
Still practising the
Second-hand thoughts of society.
Some well-spoken people can be seen
Still being unkind outside professional settings.
Some well-read people can be seen
Still supporting biassed perspectives.
Some well-respected people can be seen
Still disrespecting others without any objectives.

Call it the irony of modern times or
the hypocrisy,
Wonderful words can be repeatedly fed and
spilled with hidden motives,
But sincere actions can't be reiterated with
superficial sweetness for a lifetime.
Because actions demand character, and
The character can't be odorized with
fugacious fragrance consistently!

Economical Duality

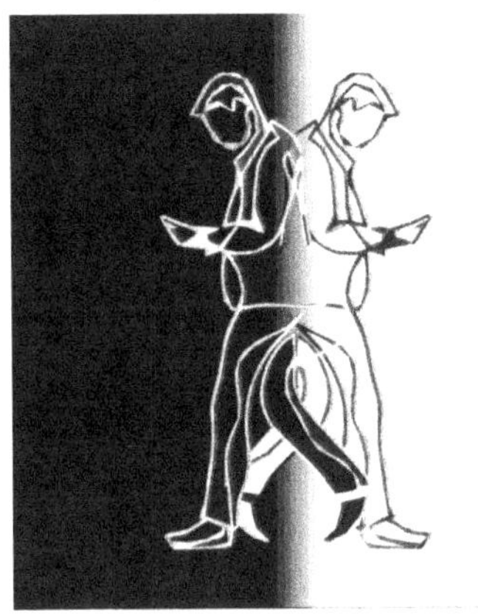

What should I say about those?
Who am I to speak of those,
Who neither understand
anything about themselves
Nor lose themselves in the teachings of God?
Who neither cry their hearts out
in front of their friends,
Nor ever laugh genuinely,
even remembered by aliens!
Who neither lost anything significant enough,
to call it a great loss,
Nor ever celebrated an insignificant gain,
which seems frivolous!

What should I say about this duality,
Which seizes our sleep almost every time?
But what a treat to be a small twig
With no worries about the destination,
Let it all come, whatever may!

What should I say about this duality,
Which seems distinct sometimes.
But always is like the bob of the pendulum—
The farther you get released from one side,
The closer you reach the opposite end.

Tell me, would you like to know
more about this duality?
Then, it is not that
The joy is better than the jeopardy, or
The achievements are
worthier than the shortcomings.
We placed them on a scale
same as positive and negative numbers,
We created our reasons to believe that it is true.
Because if failure isn't labelled as something
bad
as it's always been,
You won't pay a fortune to have that
glorious success in your pocket.

Lesson in Loss

You know, being a tree,
Is never easy.
But the way it knows life's flow,
Is a thing of beauty.
How when new leaves emerge,
It begins sending nourishment to
All those fresh addresses!
How when the fruits start to develop,
It wraps them in a protective cover,
Only allowing the birds to enjoy
their months of labour.

Then, when its parts have done their part,
When the fruits fall, and
The seeds are taken to the woods,

When the flowers droop, and
The branches remain bare,
When the leaves turn yellow, and
They eventually fall,
Know that,
The tree lives with the realism, that
Losing a few parts
Would never make the whole of it infirm.

The Rant of Race

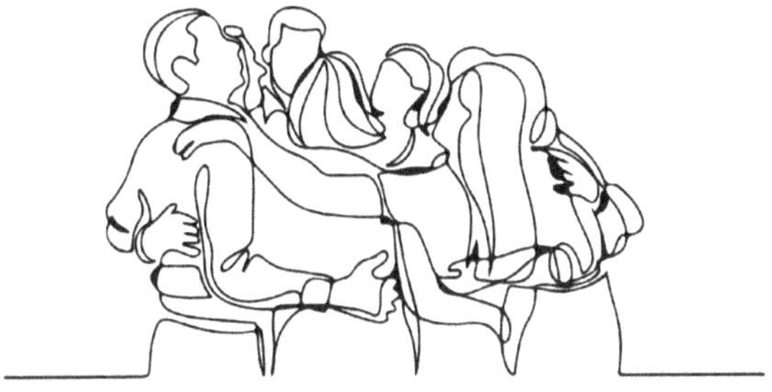

We try to save it for later,
While our present cries for now or never.
We try to seize fleeting moments with our lover,
While our friends recall our absence.
We are busy trading this for that,
Wishing we could have both,
If only we could have it, altogether.

Life runs faster than we could ever imagine,
Years are spent in blinks,
When we look back,
Decades feel like minutes.
The reality is we learn too late
to focus on ourselves—
Our priorities, our negotiables,
Our bend-or-breaks, our unacceptable.
We join the race with untied laces,
We refuse to pause, refuse to learn to tie them.
But by then, our friends become hostile,

Our lover no longer waits for our love,
Our families learn to not modify our spaces, and
And our neighbours stop asking
how our day was.
We have been in this race for so long,
that we forgot
There is no special award for finishing first here.
Maybe it was not a solo race against the world,
Maybe it's a game of cricket, or kho-kho, or
even volleyball or soccer.
The intention is, it may not be as solo
as we continue to rant,
Maybe, the real game
Is learning to play with the variables
In a way that does not ruin the constants.

Assumptions

We have assumed
Structures are equivalent to the strength within,
Outlook as a guaranteed reflection of
the being inside,
Quantities as an undoubted measure
of the luxuries, and
Money as the sole solution to
diverse adversaries.
Because we have seen scarcities,
Struggled for survival,
Craved for validations and
Cried for acceptance worldwide.

They might help, to some extent,
So, continue to assume, as you might.
But know that insecurities don't check

your bank balance
Before they decide to crawl in.
Know that fear is not afraid of the big mansion
You are living in.
Know that doubts don't dare to bother
how many cars you're driving,
Know that the heart inside you never gets to see,
If your skin is glowing.

Yes, we've lived in scarcities,
seen enough struggles,
But know that what seems apparent
Might not necessarily be evident.
You can earn the entire world's validation, or
Buy an entire island,
But peace is something that will always
come from within,
Not from running after materials,
skipping emotional growth,
Or by overlooking the pits
that you continue to carry,
Hoping your achievements would
effortlessly conceal those.

Loving Humans

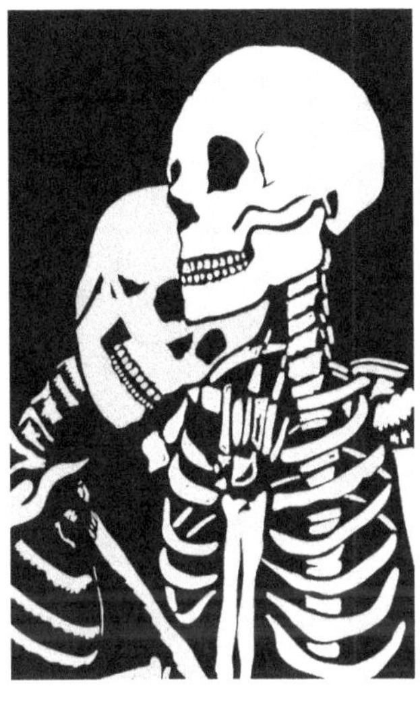

I deliberately choose what's easier—
The silence, over communication,
Distance, over inclination.
I know, that choosing the latter may mean
I need to continue to work on myself,
Like an ever-unfinished business.
But like you, I am too tired of this all.
Do you realise?
Maybe, I am not good with promises
To keep someone else happy.
I've heard that is not my responsibility
in the first place.
Maybe, I am not good at commitments

To keep for a lifetime,
Because I have seen how people often feel
More chained in such sweet relationships.
So, I let them all be,
Break these chains and
Let them breathe freely
And believe me, when I say,
How happy that makes me!
I admit that
I have been foolish enough, and
Also, loving humans is not an easy task
For the ego; nobody ever told me!

Lacuna as Favour

You can run away,
From people, from problems, from pain.
You can roam around,
In places, you have never been.
You can consume the entire feed
on your social media, or
You can binge-watch your favourite web series.
But there's a realisation that struck me
Quite counter-intuitively, recently, that
Sometimes the best way to
Stop feel something is to be in it.
Not out of it.
Be in it.
Because sometimes when you step out,
You can see how that whole thing is
split into pieces, and

How all those parts chase you,
Creating that split-second of terror,
Of sadness, of grief,
In a way like the multiples,
That grows with each calculation every time.
You can see how
You start accumulating all the emotions
you don't want to feel.
So, why run away?
Why not sit with it?
Why not face it once and for all?
Why lose those split-seconds, those millions?
During moments when sometimes we are
entirely immersed
We often miss the dots that make up those parts.
Why not use this lacuna as a favour?
Why don't we set aside fear and
simply dive in deeper?

Blessed, the Broken

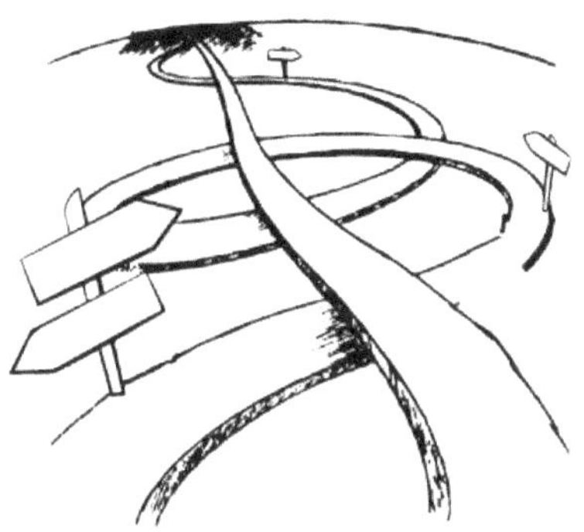

What a privilege it is
To be broken, to feel lost,
To lose something so dear,
To see silently, the death of your prayers,
Yet still find your way back to another version.
As they say,
The light enters through the slits in your heart.
But I'd add if you are lucky enough
to be completely shattered,
It does not just illuminate;
It bathes all your broken parts.
As you might know,
Those who never interrogate,
Never lose sleep searching for answers.
But I'd add if you dare to question
your entire journey,
Even the momentary stops will reveal

hints to ponder.
As we are accustomed to mourn those
we've lost,
I'd remind you what a luxury it is
to cherish these little moments we've got.
As we are habituated to assign blame,
whether to God or humans
I'd love to remind, that sometimes
all you can do is pray,
Yet your faith should not waver
based on the outcome.

So, I'll repeat,
What a privilege it is
To be broken, to feel lost,
To lose something so dear,
To silently witness the death of your prayers,
Yet still find your way back to another version.
It's like being the boomerang in God's hand,
You don't know how far you've been thrown or
with what intentions!
But you just know
The pull towards God is strong.
You just know you will return home,
You wouldn't be forever lost.

As an Unknown

I've travelled to places, and
Lived in cultures
Way different than my own.
Yet, I've never felt like an outsider.
Because, to feel like
You don't belong,
You must belong somewhere already.
To feel like the odd one out,
You have to know who you are and
The ones who even you out.

I might have never known myself,
In a way, that prevents me to be with others.

Perhaps, that was a blessing in disguise.
So, every place I went,
Always felt like home!
It never bothered me,
If I was different,
Or if I was alone!

Social Feed

Indeed, the biggest boons can turn into
the worst banes too,
No matter the reason,
Nothing could escape this pattern,
Including social media, that we use recklessly.
Because when we create things that are
unlimited by nature,
We need to know how to limit ourselves better.
Be it those calls, or shares, or posts, or scrolls,
We need to define a personal threshold.
But, if you look at it in moderation,
You can see the good it brings:
People learn
How to make their little moments count,
Regardless of whether
they capture and post it or not.
People learn to smile through their struggles,
Even for just a few seconds,

Yes, that funny reel you shared didn't go in vain.
We learnt to laugh at our adversities,
Through those relatable memes
That made fun of our stupidities!
How people come up with words like
'Cat mom' or 'Book babies'
You may call it an exaggeration,
But I'd choose to see
how they reached the core emotion.
We learned that if not a heartfelt conversation,
Then sending a heart-touching video is enough,
To remind the people we love, that
We may not know all about them, but
We hope they get the courage to push through it
slowly, over time.
Yes, no matter how much they are mocked,
Motivational posts have a way of
clearing our mental blocks.
*At the end of the day, it's those laughter
and the love reactions
That make us feel so worthy, by connecting us
with our go-to emotions.*

Phoenix within Fireflies

I see my transformations
Over these years, and
Let me walk you through those
If you've come this far.
You saw how my toxicity
Made me offer silent treatment to my God,
How in the most challenging times
I could never believe in the power of prayers.
I've visited temples, seen the deities,
My anger was too high,
I never bent for any blessings.
I was busy asking the questions in my mind
Which won't serve anything.
I was too lost in connecting the dots,

I never noticed
If all those dots actually mattered.
I had been too self-reliant,
As asking for help always comes with a price,
sooner or later.
I have been the proudest nerd,
You can make fun, but I realise now,
how it catered.
Had been too dumb to understand
some clever jokes,
Or the ulterior motive behind
some sweet gestures.
I found out,
Though people can walk with you in the dark,
But when you hit the rock-bottom
You're all alone, my dear.

Yes, a few things do happen
beyond your control,
But they cannot and will not stop
what is destined to happen.
The days I spent working
on my ideas of whys and the hows,
The nights I stayed awake
wishing to have my faith restored,
The evenings I spent meditating,
The mornings I tried practising gratitude,
overlooking the doubts.
A clueless heart has

the world's most difficult power,
It gathers the courage to do so much,
without expecting anything in return,
Without getting attached, and so, without hurt.
Maybe that's how
He plants the seed of detachment,
When 'I' was busy doing everything
'I' had loved ever,
But couldn't remember anything,
Because 'I' was not noticing
anything in particular.

Then, the dots started connecting themselves,
The questions were eventually answered,
'I' changed, for the sake of my 'self',
I stopped looking, and
they somehow started to appear.
Oh, the volume of tears you shed to shed the
older version of yourself!
The heap of trust you need to restart
with all you've learnt,
Like the Phoenix that rises from the ashes,
Like the fireflies that never forget
to glow in the dark after rain.

Yes, 'I' changed,
The one people have known
at some point in my journey,
She might have existed once, but

unapologetically, she exists no more.

Then came this side of me,
The spirit of the Phoenix within
the spirit of the fireflies, and
If you think you can bottle me up
to watch me glowing,
Know that I will break your jar,
And set your whole house on fire.

Yet, a few things I decided to keep unchanged,
How I still take long breaks for 12 hours
After working for the previous 8!
I believe I've been this cute always,
I just never remember to look at the mirror
in your eyes.

Singularity of Self-love

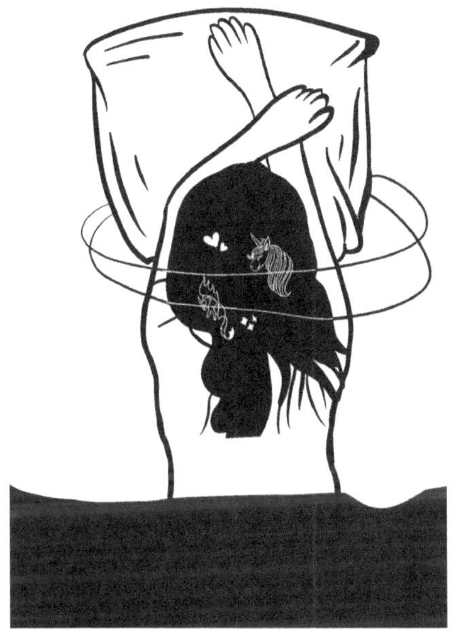

What a tragedy it has been
All these years of being everything
That people and situations demanded of me
Yet, neglecting my deeper yearnings!
What a tragedy,
Until a flood of new notions came
That shook people awake from their slumber.
Humans and their clever ways
of designing societies,
Always glorified things with hidden motives,

To make people believe, that
Yes, only this is what ultimately matters.
Be it love, marriage, having kids, or grandkids.
Be it the social acceptance, following the mass,
Or getting popular validations
only to emphasise that
It's not yours, but rather only others' opinions
that truly matter.

What a tragedy!
Isn't it?
Or should I say, what a clever plot!
You never had to bother about yourself
But try your entire life to fit into some moulds.

It took us several decades
To arrive there, where the new notion of
Self-love secures the same spot,
Where we are trying to create an idea
That sounds as poetic as romantic love,
As essential as marriages once were, and
As ineffable as giving birth.
Yet they also become incomplete
When you try to
Make it the only ultimate goal for everyone.

How can we decide for the whole
When the parts are whole on their own?
How can we decide for others

When we struggle with our personal decisions?

I hope you can figure out the words spoken
Are just individual opinions and
You are allowed to have yours,
With or without validations.
You are allowed to live your life,
Be it with self-love or in selfless service, or
anything else, and
For others, it really does not matter.
As long as the parts
involved in your part are content,
The discontentment of the whole outsiders
simply shatters.

I cannot deny,
How in this mesh of multiple marathons
I also forgot to meditate on myself,
Which is why you might think
I'm new on this track of self-love.
But people who've been doing it
for some time now,
Might not explicitly utter these words,
Might have found the balance
Between the self and the outside world.
*You know, another tragedy is, how in the craze
for singularity,
Even the greatest and most harmless ideas
lose their worth.*

Implications

In my most honest attempts
To be myself,
Without causing any confusion in others,
It still has been a failure to communicate that
Every criticism is not hatred, and
Every act of affection is not romantic love.
It has been a failure
in friendships
to make people believe that
I can criticise them,
Without any intentions of disrespect,
Without any wish to bring them down,
Without any desire to question their existence.
Yet, if they choose to grow and learn,
Know that I seek no selfish gain
From their choices in my mind,

Know that if I want the good for them only, and
never for me
Then let it be just that,
Without trying to establish
How one emotion
should also implicate in another,
Without trying to impose on me
The misunderstandings they enjoy inferring
From my clear communications.

From my honest experiences
I've realised that
If, to keep a fearful peace,
I have to unwillingly choose silence,
Those were never healthy friendships for me
in the first place.

Utopian Wish

We have seen countries declaring wars,
We have seen kingdoms indulging in combats,
Taking pride in their victories, and
Feeling saddened by their defeats.
But, everything is based on the sole condition
It's always our side that
We should be supporting.
Irrespective of the fairness,
Judgements, circumstances,
Morals and ethics,
It has always felt easier
To raise voices against others,
Even when our side was duly questionable.
Because we somehow learnt

We are better than them,
Even if it's injustice that we're supporting.
Because we somehow forgot that
people among us
Might also support the vicious.
We created a crowd, and called that community,
We decided to do the right,
in the name of divinity,
But diluted its meaning
in our deep personal prejudices.

What can be more painful than
Seeing humans killing humans
Yet taking pride in their acts?
What can be more disheartening than
Watching families getting recognition
For the lives their dear ones have lost?
No, I would never wish that pain on anyone.
What good is our education?
What good is our religion?
What good is our patriotism, technologies, or
spirituality?
If we cannot practise basic humanity!
How can we agree to any pride
That comes after knowing
Martyrs lose their lives
On the borders of their own countries?
Wasn't the country also supposed to protect
them?

How can we agree to any education
That could not teach us
about respecting boundaries?
Why can't we control our greed to invite peace?
How can we agree to any religion
Which tries to impose itself and
misguide people into killing others?
Why can't we understand that
We won't deserve heaven after
creating hell for uncountable individuals?
How can we agree to any patriotic feeling
Which lets us forget our inner being
and makes us show only conditional compassion
For people belonging to "my community"?

Why can't we realise that
Looking down
on other countries doesn't make us any greater?
How can we agree to any technology
Which makes us feel superior
in being a little more inhuman
In our attempts to invade or protect our
boundaries?
Why can't we sign real treaties and
follow them strictly?
How can we agree to any form of spirituality
Which boosts our ego of dominance,
and monopoly?
Why don't we understand

If we don't have control over ourselves,
We cannot attempt to control the mass?

I know it's a long battle for each one of us,
Full of manipulated histories,
and biassed numbers.
But my utopian view excludes
the need for wars and soldiers,
I'd pray people come home alive,
Be it acquaintances or strangers.
I'd pray people get to live their lives,
Without being a sacrifice to
someone else's mistakes.
I wish our boundaries were
for smooth regulations, and
Not a shield against the threats
That we love creating for each other.
I'd wish besides advancing on so many fronts,
We go back, to realise and recalculate,
How much of humanity we lost
In the name of religion or patriotism.

The human world is strangely pathetic,
We can't save lives,
But we believe in biassed killing.
In my utopian world,
I see the country protecting its countrymen,
People doing their best without bringing the
worst to anyone,

Everything and everyone exists
Without trying to prove that
They are everything the world needs,
Their beliefs are what can transform the world,

I pray for a nation,
Where no mother's son would have
his last breath on the battlefield,
No young girl would become a widow for life,
No children would have to salute a corpse
wrapped in a national flag.
I'd pray, we could
find a solution other than ammunition.

Girls like Us

There are girls
Who have composed the music of their life
During moments of solitude,
While the devils were busy playing
Tantrums in their minds and lives.
They have consciously attuned their life
To their dreams and desires, day and night.

Girls who could have chosen
To sit and cry about their situations,
Seek love and attention,
As they often say, girls do,
I have seen the same in many,

Irrespective of not being a girl.
But, these girls choose to cry
Not to get any favour,.
But to let the pain out,
And then they sit with their dreams,
Until the devils burn out.

These girls, who learnt to take
The oar in their hands and
Row their little boats,
Through smooth waters and raging storms;
Not wishing for someone else
to dictate their route.
Because while people feel they are helpless,
Tempting them with an assurance of help
hardly works.
The ill-intentions of people are
eventually exposed.
So, if you ever lent someone help
looking selfishly for some applause,
Your little contributions to their life,
won't make you their Lord!
Let me repeat, in case you missed it,
These are the girls
Who have composed the music of their life
During moments of solitude,
While the devils were busy playing
Tantrums in their minds and lives.
They have consciously attuned their life

To the ebbs and flows, day and night.
Your promises of anything
Is insignificant to them,
When they know they can
Write the poems of their life.

If you feel she is a trophy,
You need to pursue until you win,
Because you see her struggles and achievements
As your keys to a comfortable life.
Then, let me burst the bubble for
All the girls out there:
They never entertain free rides.
They have their choices and opinions, and
If they say "NO" for once and for all,
It doesn't matter if you say "YES"
a thousand times!
Knowing what she wants,
she can find her way out.
She is not waiting for a saviour!
She doesn't enjoy only sitting and crying,
you know.
Because she knows she is not stuck
to be rescued,
By people who don't yet know
since when they've been lost.

We are too busy saying this helplessly that
Things meant for us, always find us,

Almost overlooking,
Not everything finding us
Is necessarily meant for us.

Roaming for Home

People are often mistaken,
By the souls generous in their demeanour,
Generous beyond they should be,
Generous without even knowing
When to draw boundaries.

People are mistaken,
To see that as an opportunity to
Explore and exploit.
They believe whatever they assume to be true.
The lost and hopeless people

Who just need any anchor to avoid the
Harsh waves of life.
Selfish, and narcissistic people
Who only care for their happiness since
They enjoy being victims.
The "I'm your friend for life" and
"I'm not like others" people
Who want your friendship
Merely as a comfortable distraction in their
so-called painful life.

These people have a tendency
To be mistaken by the
Uncalculated affection and
non-transactional emotions
You share with them,
Like you share with everyone else.
People who take no responsibilities
to live in reality, rather
Make you live in their falsified fantasies,
Because they make you a place to take rest,
While demanding all the warmth of a home.
These people have a tendency
To think that,
Affection and care always imply
An absence of discernment, and
A lifetime of permit to some dreamland.

These people roam from heart to heart
To find and claim someone as
their own.
Every time you act humanely with them,
They think, "Yes, you're the one."
This cycle of roaming and resting continues
With every generous human being
they come across,
Intentionally hurting some hearts along the way
To their justified self-centred happiness.
But they don't settle.
They can't, because,
They don't know exactly where they are broken.
They don't know,
Love does not magically change life, and
Their ignorance has too big an ego
to accept that.
They don't know,
Love is never forced upon others and
If they need the other person
Solely for their satisfaction,
Then it was never love, ever.
They don't know,
Out of all the ways to hurt you,
Silencing your opinions is the loudest
To prove how genuinely they don't know
how to love you.

These people,
I wish, would come with a warning
"Handle being aware"!
Because no matter how carefully you manage
They can create havoc and wrench your heart.
But in their mayhem, they forget,
That just because you are generous
Does not imply you are not aware!
Does not imply you would never
close the doors!
And never stop showing care.
They forget—where there is kindness
There can be sternness too.
Where there are certain permits
There are several restrictions too.
If they cannot respect your "NO,"
You can firmly reject their "Yes" too.

Be it you, or be it them,
Don't try to turn every place of rest into a home.
In your attempt to claim people as your wins,
You forgot it was only you in the first place
Who selfishly started and
blindly continued to roam.
NO,
You can't dream of having people
Whose generosity you've consciously ruined.
So, don't try to make me your home
with such hopes.

I know the journey I'm on,
might look attractive to you,
But the cycle of people coming and going,
will continue, and
I'd never regret,
If I consciously choose to lose you!

In Love

I know, I might not be 'beautiful'
The way you think about those words.
I don't spend hours lightening or
Brightening my skin colour,
Just to hear these nine letters
In the same sequence as I've written.
That doesn't help much maybe, is all I believe.
'Cause I'm so dissolved in something that
You'd never notice or praise.
Rather criticise, if you can't do the same.

But I try to notice and love them,
As they say I should, because
they're truly mine:
The split ends of my hair,
The almost crescent dark moons under

The infinity formed by my eyes,
The blunt thing called a nose in between them,
The chapped lips,
The fatty deposits around my waist,
The threads wrapped around my wrist for years,
The invariable ponytail which I prefer,
My instability in wearing high heels,
The tears I shed in pain of losing my dears,
The not-so-big things
that make me shrink in fear, or
Overthinking things and wasting my time,
They are all mine.

All my meaningless metaphors that make my
Didi laugh,
The scoldings which make my Maa wanting to
be my daughter,
Little sensibilities that make my Baba proud,
The affection that makes my friends dance and
cry out.
The rarely-expressed but sometimes-cared
broken, incomplete,
Damaged, imperfect elements which make me
complete,
I am in love with them all.
I know, beautiful is good, but
How can I be that beautiful?
I cannot be just that.

Failed Success

People say,
If you fall in love.
There is a chance,
You might also
Fail in it.
But wait—
Does that mean,
Love is an achievement?
Something that brings you either success
or a setback?
Then, is love-marriage like our success stories
Which glorify and boast about

our hard work only?
How can we preach love as the biggest truth
If, in hindsight, it is only our ego
that we are boasting?

I do not know,
So, I'd rather leave it to you.
I think when we start to see ourselves
Bigger than the processes, or
Greater than the events,
Then we are bound to miss the real joys,
We're sure to
overshadow the salience of the substance.

Why Sacrifice?

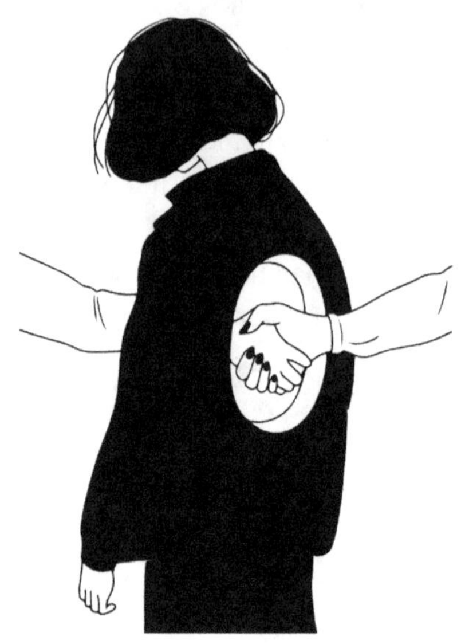

No matter how much of the world's greatness
Lies entirely in the
Acts of sacrifice,
I'd like to argue,
Definitely,
Not being a distinct person of intellect,
Rather, as a simple, ordinary person
Who does not understand the
Complications we deliberately introduce
To make things appear desirable
in the eyes of a noob.

I have seen people solve bigger problems
Simply by changing the ways of their thinking,
I have seen adamance learning humbleness
Through just a shift in perspectives.
So, people say things like,
"This has never happened in our family," or
"Our place is not open to these things," and
They also feel proud saying,
"I'd love to be like that, but
I'd have to give up my dreams".
Be it that business, that skill, that person, or
that new thinking,
I've seen these people always finding ways
To not act, even before considering
the ways they could've tried.
I know sacrifices are necessary sometimes, and
I don't deny the amount of detachment it invites,
but
*Some sacrifices are just the unwillingness
to do what's truly desired and
Accepting the easy defeat,
While comfortably calling ourselves helpless,
in the hands of fate.*

The New Class

I'd been the brightest in the class,
Only to discover later that
I might have been in the wrong class!
Only to realise later that
I was never fully present in them.
I'd been avoidant, and hard to teach.
But because I always enjoyed studying alone,.
Not because I was running away from wisdom.
But because I found a profound peace in
Uncovering the meanings on my own.
And because I enjoyed
How the phrases formed even before
I knew if they made sense.

But ever since
I started being the opposite,
I've begun enjoying the classes.
I'm surprised
How so many people are eager to share
Their hard-earned knowledge
without feeling insecure
That you might surpass them, and
That has critically changed the game!

I think this is the class I would like to spend
The rest of my life in,
Without erasing the abilities,
the former has ushered.

Living Death

I wish I could witness
Death dying and
Life thriving
Through bare bodies
Of flesh and bones,
Rather, to be real, only bones.

Those nightmares I watched with
Eyes wide open,
Fearing if that was the night
I was going to lose him forever.
How loud and long were those seconds,
When prayers and fears co-existed,
In the most deadly dance of duality.
In one moment, I'd suffocate myself
With the delicate existence of life, and

In another, I'd wish to
Burn all those imaginary cords,
Running through my mind,
Blocking my throat.
I was oscillating for hope,
But it seemed like something,
I could never afford.

Somehow, the mornings would come.
The only gratitude I could express was:
Thank God, this night has passed, and
This was not 'that' night!
I don't know how the conditionings work,
But they worked.
The bustling sounds in the morning—
Of kids shouting while getting ready for school,
Their moms reassuring
If they'd taken the lunchbox, and
Dads reminding them
how little time they've got
Before it's too late to reach.
The daylight did seem lighter,
Hope was easier to find in this familiar noise,
Until the nights returned,
With their familiar loneliness and poise.
And let me tell you, a little too harshly that
No matter how busier the days were, with
Accompaniments and accomplishments,
The nights were always this challenging,

As an inevitable battle to win.
I was cast as a soldier,
Without support.
At times, I'd see phosphenes
Wondering who was my real enemy.
There were too many on the other side –
My fear, the irreversible truth, the logic,
His disease, his weakening body,
the complex side-effects, and
Among them, there was God,
To transform all of them into a miracle
That would serve as the only support
On my side.
I still don't know where to place God
In this non-algebraic equation of death and life,
Amid this panorama of
Human emotions in-between.

Nevertheless, I was certain,
He was not with me, with him, or with us.
When reality is too heavy to bear,
Disbelief feels effortless to exercise.

Some nights, I'd wonder,
If I was wishing for something impractical,
illogical, and irrational
When I could see Death sleeping at our home
fearlessly.
But, are prayers supposed to be practical?

I know, there is no one-word answer, but
Only the ones
with terms and conditions attached.
Let me tell you, a little too harshly, that
Prayers do fail and
The sooner you prepare yourself for this truth,
The easier peace can find you.
Well, I do not know the magical mix of prayers
To make it pass all exams for being real,
But it was difficult to feel their power
In those nights, and the days thereafter.

He was relieved, but his pain could not be cured.
Wished for the disease to decease,
But was tricked by the plans of God—
To know my fears, He made me pray.
I did, fearfully indeed.
At last, the fear won, and prayers were lost.

If Death is another face of God,
Then God also won that battle.
I could never believe He was on our side,
He proved how I was never wrong,
all those times.

Boundaries & Beyond

When Silence Speaks

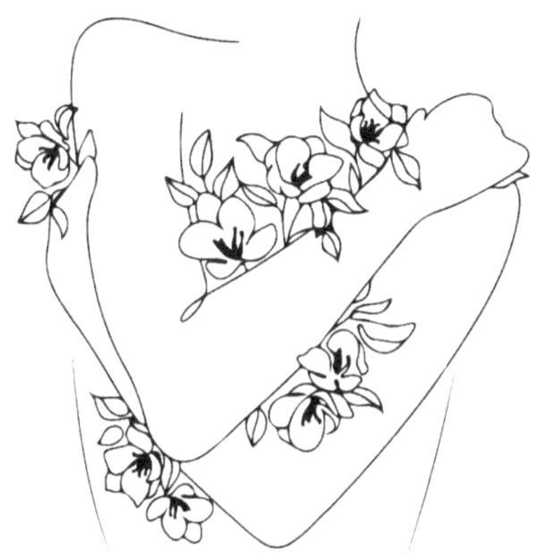

I choose to think about it this way, that
The Universal Silence speaks to us,
Through these compositions.
Because every time I try to say something,
Either it is about clashes, criticisms,
Or complaints and even comparisons.
It is rarely around contentment.
But look at the times that
Fathomless Infinity speaks,
See how duties feel like service,
See how even the gruelling lessons
feel gentle and genuine, and
I do not know which is more unequalled,
Carrying this gift of translating the
Infinite Silence, or receiving it!

I might say both for ideal equality, but
Inherently, I am inclined towards
the ones receiving it.
Because I happen to be there also,
Enjoying so many people's gifts, and
I feel it is no less than any milestone,
To find your unexceptional expressions in
someone else's evident reflections!

Captured without Pictures

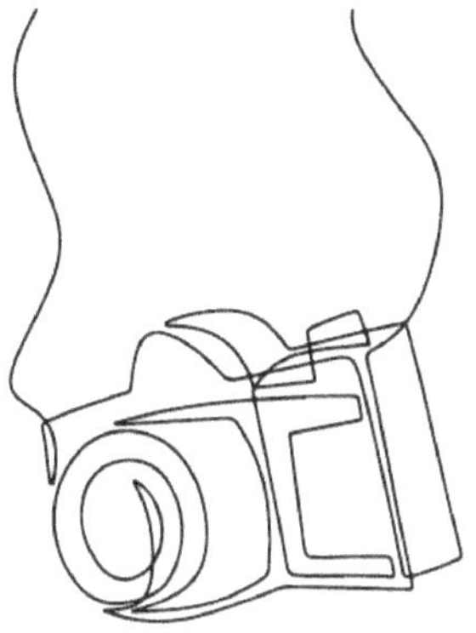

It is so strangely beautiful that
Sometimes, we don't have a single picture
With the people we love,
If not most, then at least, not the least too.
Not even a blurry blink is captured with them
Amidst this endlessly fleeting time.

Instead, we learn to preserve a part of them
In countless other tiny pixels:
In the colour of our special wear,
In a fraction of our hesitant glance,
In the invisible smile of our soul
That doesn't touch our lips,
Yet we feel like
Witnessing a thousand blossoms.
Only then we do learn, that

A photograph is not the only way to capture
A moment, some memories, and
minutes of meetings.
The serene silence of our smiles
can also put together
The pixels slipped off our hesitant eyes.
The way we let our few moments be worthless
By not looking at their face, knowing,
We are being looked at, in a manner,
possibly worthier and more loving;
The way we sweetly sacrifice our wish
to be heard
To feel the aliveness in their voice, and
Many other such bytes,
beyond our usual ways of framing;
*We learn to capture them
in the unadulterated split of a second,
With our senses, with no proof of how much love
they continue to send.*

My Definition

I've filled pages
In my diary,
Which then kept hidden, carefully,
With poems that didn't seem to end.
I doubt,
I had a habit of extending
Things beyond their natural extent.
But wait.
I suppose,
That was a harsh comment
By me on myself.
So, I'd make some corrections:
I might have known
How to lengthen the life of compositions.

Getting back,
My poems refused to end.
God knows how much time I had spent.
Then, once I heard someone say,
"Fewer words, worthier," and
Believe me,
I set all the pages ablaze.
I found no meaning in my extended rhymes;
I felt no attachment
To what all along had been.

Years passed
In learning this difficult skill—
How to shrink the volume of my pages
To just a few lines.
Somehow it came to me,
Albeit not naturally.
Yet I took pride in my work
For doing it lovingly.

I heard people saying again,
"Oh, such small stanzas
Are never called poems."

But this time, thankfully,
I've explored willingly;
Didn't try to tame my words
When all they wanted was to be free.
Didn't try to fit them into a mould,

Didn't panic if they failed to rhyme;
Nor did I try to shrink them needlessly
Just to conform to a definition!
Now that you know about my old self,
You know, how restrictions hardly work for me.

So, I wrote,
Sometimes with pause, sometimes in flow.
Like this:
Some lines with two,
Some lines with four.
If you wish, call it poetry.
Maybe just give it a go.
But if you don't feel so,
Just let it be.
Because maybe then, it's just me!
Not your usual poetry.

Curse of the Blessed

We know the power of
Love and light,
But also realise,
They can't wipe away
All the darkness of the nights,
When you think in terms of the world,
Even the good cannot impose itself
On the critical.

I have tried in vain,
To bring people out of their pain.
While I didn't realise that,
I was blinded by the light!
I have believed in positivity,
A way too optimistically,
Until I found peace in the fact, that
Not everyone wanted to be saved;
Not everyone drowns

due to a lack of external aid.
Some just choose to cling to the pain,
As a way to receive the opposite,
as it does often.
What I learned, from my intentions
to be a good human,
Is to see if the person genuinely wants
to be helped.
To see, if the person sincerely loves the light,
Or if they're just overjoyed to get a free ride.
I've seen people cursing the ones
Who've prayed for their well-being.
I've heard people questioning,
"Did I ask you to do so?"
When they lived a blessing
They could never believe it was possible,
not even in their distant dreams!
Yes, love and light might not be there
within your everyday sights.
Somedays, you might consciously need to
put them aside.
*If you work to build a stable kingdom for
yourself, learn to exercise your might!*

Secret about Happiness

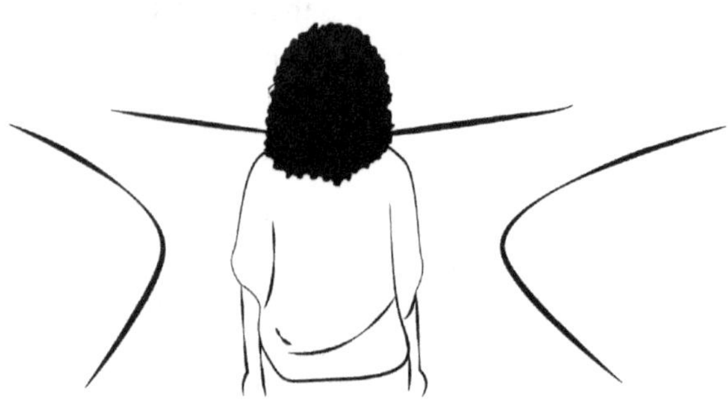

There is something deeply disquieting
about that happiness—
The kind which becomes your goal,
Makes you pray all day and night long,
Lets your entire existence revolve around its
pursuit,
And keeps you awake until achieved.
That happiness
That rules your life,
And decides what you have is nothing.
That happiness
Has a deeply disturbing quality,
You might not recognise it
unless you have lived it.

The same happiness that feels like
a missing heartbeat, and
Makes you question

if your fulfilment is authentic;
Also dispenses you with a sense of detachment
the moment you finally embrace it.

I assume there is a secret puzzle behind
granting happiness.
I assume I have figured it out.
Every time I made it 'dreamy and special'
It only made me impatient and doubtful.
Only if you too have longed for something
for so long,
Only if you too have wondered whether wishing
for it is right or wrong,
Only if you too have pedalled the cycle of
belief and cynicism,
You might've embodied
What's in achieving that—and what if it is gone?

Every time I made it my utmost necessity,
I noticed how my life remained nonchalant,
almost!
*I assume our idea of happiness
has been incomplete;
Life goes on with or without it!*

Limitations in Love

It's heartwarming to utter these words, that
Friendships taught me the best things about love.
They said, "If you truly love love,
then never make it the reason for
your not-doings, or your not-beings."
What did they mean by that?
Read this slowly, as I have already bookmarked.
We tend to overlook,
When we are completely immersed.

Be it poems, or be it love,
There is always a need for some space,
As I have kept some above.
But this is not what they stated.

People often say with pride,
"I cannot do this, as
I am now in this relationship."
Partially, you can be justified,

As you've some new titles in your personal life.
But how saddening would it feel,
If you make that sweet bond a brutal excuse
subconsciously?
An excuse for not being what you wish to be;
A reason why you can't act
how you think you should;
A reason why you feel obliged
to put everyone else first
While your dreams, your individuality,
Your choices and expressions take a backseat
silently.
Often, people don't restrict us,
But, we proudly put these chains
around ourselves and
Try to call it love!
If it is imposed,
Where is the freedom in it?
If it does not ask your opinion,
Where are your interests in it?

Nobody said,
The butterfly has to give up its colours
To pollinate the flowers.
Rather, it transforms itself.
It leaves the cocoon gracefully.

There is this fine line that separates
A bond from being a bondage.
The former helps you grow.
The latter is insecure about
your colourful change!

So, if you truly love love, or
Wish to be loved truthfully,
Be free enough to set yourself free
To live the life of your sweet dreams,
To work for that life consistently.
Otherwise, how contradictory would it be
For you to make yourself empty
Just to pour your love persistently?

They said love is not your limitation, sweetheart,
Love does not ask for your wings!
The birth of love is not
the death of your dreams.

Dreaming, not Sleeping

So, when I say,
I like to live in my dreams,
I do not mean
I wish to remain asleep.
I mean, to open my eyes and
Sense my dreams awakening
The rush in the morning,
The delight in the delays
On my way, and
The guilty pleasure of the prohibited naps
In between.

When I say,
I like to smile in my dreams,
I do not mean

I wish to scare the person lying by my side.
Rather, I mean to
Spread my lips knowing
That I do have the courage
To kiss the adversities and
To wink at the difficulties,
Of course, only after I'm done crying.

I can go on and on like this, although,
I already see you've got my little rhyme.

Take a Trip

Either you book your tickets
and propel your feet
or
You take your book and
explore the world
from the comfort of your couch.

Homes of Art

Every piece of art
That is birthed by you
Is already destined for a place
In this world
You know nothing about.

So, it is both beautiful and profound,
To know that
A home is not just the place of birth
For any piece of art,
But also the many unknown addresses
To which it travels and
Leaves a lasting lustre
Of which the parent knows nothing about.

So, when you doubt if it is worth
To let this art be born,
Just remember that a home is waiting for
That seemingly insignificant stroke to house.

Literal Legends

In a world full of
Conditions in a so-called unconditional love,
Came this stranger
Who knew me by face and so did I.
In a world full of
Virtual closeness amid real distances,
Was this stranger
Who knew nothing about me and neither did I.
Yet, in a world full of daily loops and routines
This stranger was there,
Like one of those numerous people
We pass by without ever saying hi!
Although we do have some assumptions
about their life
From the clues we happily carry,
In our conversations and costumes of all types.

This stranger was there,
Just like I might have also been for them.

Until one day, when that silence broke, and
What could be more beautiful than some
Sweet gestures that show
How big of a heart such strangers hold.

First conversation, without words.
One glance to let me know that
This stranger cares.
One selflessly successful act of saving a seat
for me in the swamped public bus.
One morning of filling my only heart
with the love of a thousand hearts.

The second conversation, a thank you
Whispered near that person's ears.
Was it the last too? I don't know,
But this one felt blessed enough.

Within the next few moments,
the stranger was gone.
And left me sitting there, writing a poem.
No, you don't write poems for people
for the same reasons.
Some to erase the hurt
from your heart forever
By scratching the spotless skin of a paper.

Some to remind yourself
How far you've come and
How far to go from there.
Some to save the naughty memories and
the nostalgic moments
With the people we know,
with the people we love, and
Some like this one,
To share the sheer selflessness
some strangers show and
Win a big home in our heart.

'Cause if there are some chains
which don't need to be broken,
It's these chains of kindness,
That don't wait to expect anything in return.
If there are people who need to be mentioned,
then it's these people,
Who are the unsung legends in our
unnamed stories of daily survival.

Not to Know

I often catch myself thinking about
The scenarios born from fear.
The morning has just registered itself
In my consciousness and
Oh! The crowd of those moments is
already there,
Eagerly waiting for my attention,
As if so dire.
If you drag me to walk a five-hundred metre
I'd resist then and there.
But these thoughts, especially these tricky ones,
Somehow know how to bribe me,
At any minute of the hour.

Ten minutes passed, haven't opened my eyes.
Yet my mind is running at a speed
I can't match with steps, clear and concise.

Suddenly, a stream of light flashes,
Out of nowhere.

I start to think, as if with each negative thought,
I am choosing a whole new boat to sit in.
I find myself on many boats
Which take me across this river
In no time!
"So, can I step off any boat
if I wish?"
I ask my surroundings.
The answer is evident,
You don't need to close your eyes to realise.
But here is it, if you need it stated explicitly:
Having a bulk of information is no longer
the metric of intelligence, nowadays.
True knowledge is to know what not to know,
by priority or by choice.

Powerless Power

Our conception of power feels
Incomplete without experiencing this,
That the tighter you try to hold,
The weaker your grip, it reveals!

Unguaranteed Glitters

Isn't it strange, that
We all can feel
How happily everyone is living?
Be it on the social media,
Or in a social gathering.
With their heartiest captions or travel highlights,
With the so-called show-offs or
Their inputs to a social cause.
Yet, not even a glimpse of the pain
They endure
During their demise.
Yes, their demise.
Just a silent nudge to
Our attitude towards shines and spotlights,
That an attractive life here never guarantees
A painless death likewise.

Light & Vague

I am filling more air inside me
Of light and vague things—
Things which don't carry any weight of
importance,
Still can offer so much essence,
incomparable otherwise.

I am thinking about the people
Who still believe poems are only about
broken hearts!
Perhaps they never got lost in the clouds,
Never gazed at the night sky.
Never felt the wind walking all over their skin
With closed eyes and
Never listened to a baby's languageless cry.
I have nothing against them, but
My heart does ache at this belief.
So, as they say, with my broken heart,
I continue to write.

But I do think,
Those are not light and vague,
In the sense of being weightless and worthless.
Rather their lightness might symbolise hope, and
Their vagueness might mean
They are present everywhere.
But we never feel them the way we should,
As we try our best to feel their weight, and
Try to centre our focus,
instead of looking for it all around.

Social Trap

The day you realise that
All these things are nothing
And nothing can be everything,
But little bubbles in the air
Which can burst anytime—
You will stop restricting the peripheries of
Realities and possibilities.

Then it'll strike one day that,
It was all about unseeing the utterly visible and
Looking deep through things
Invisible to the open eyes.
The inescapable realisation that

The walls that protect our bodies,
still scare our souls,
We are still afraid of the depth
our truths can hold and
So frightened of the thoughts that
run naked in our inner world.
The peculiar paradox that
We are unbound social animals;
Neither are we caged,
Nor are we as free as the wild.
We are trapped by our thoughts.
We live in our safe prison,
We love calling it our home,
Our community, our society and
Scare those who try to break free and roam.

Swapped Wh's

The discussions in human society
Change the objectives, sprucely subjectively.
Last night, I was with this group of strangers,
Talking about great ideas, and thoughts
that run deeper,
Reflecting on common people, daily habits,
Their choices and their perspectives.
One striking pattern registered in my mind,
Which smoothly segregated our intentions
Even if it felt a little unkind.
For great people, we were in confusion about
'Who' said that?
Was it that poet or that philosopher?
Someone from this place or a state in my
neighbourhood?
Is he from a sect lesser known, or
Is he my community fellow?
The willingness to establish connections
with strangers
Who never know us in their living years!

The clever silence to hide any similarity
With the same,
If their acts had not been so worthy,
Displayed how helplessly
we appreciate associating
With noteworthy things, just to feel proud of
ourselves,
Or to get more validation for our proud origins.
But, when it comes to conversations about
common people,
We never care about the speaker.
We argue, and we question
'What' was being said of someone!
Someone we closely know,
Or distantly wish to know the whereabouts of.
But I feel, in reality,
We should swap the wh's
to enjoy the echt essence.

Current's Faults

There is this little trick
That notoriously tantalises
our innocent moments,
Which is this single habit of believing
That the better was behind us or
The best lies downstream always.
So we pretermit the present,
Assuming it's not a loss,
Thinking it would be recovered without regrets.
But, the nostalgia that nestles in the past,
starts to fade slowly and
The promises of the prospective
seem implausible to marry.
So, we invite the heap of hopelessness here
in this instant and
Blame the currents for making our current
excruciating to carry!

Poverty of Humanity

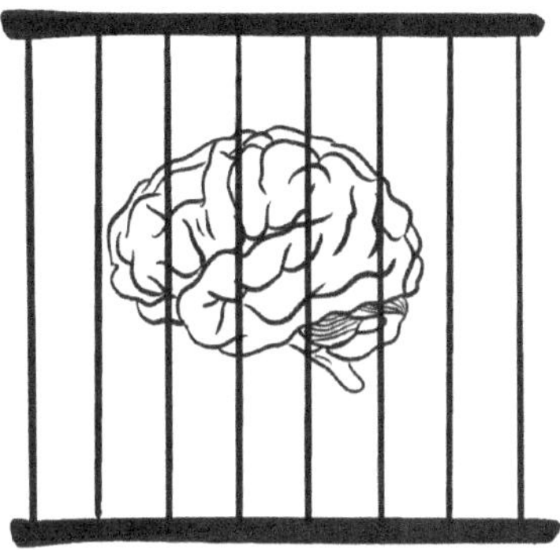

Abolish the poverty of essentials—food, shelter,
Clothes, education, and all other fundamentals.
But also demolish the poverty of humanity
Found among some rich, and
some educated alike.
What if the rest can effortlessly follow?

Fear

The journey through fear
Has been the most interesting of them all.
When I thought there was always a danger
There always existed one.

When I thought, it was the opposite of faith,
As in, a separate, individual existence,
I only saw my faith diminished, and
fear getting stronger.
As I only focused on the negative,
I believed in its power.

When I thought, the help was outside,
As some God, as some divine being,
I only felt alone,
I only saw myself fighting.
As I believed things other than me could
solve it,
I witnessed things outside me
causing all the troubles.

Until I learnt, what it is to embody strength,
I never fully felt that power within myself.
Until I learnt, which is fear is also faith,
I never saw my fears dying completely.
Until I learnt, that accepting the truth
had been easier,
I never realised how hard I tried
to resist unnecessarily.

I had seen fear sleepwalking in my dreams,
Only to wake up the strength
that sleeps within me.

Worthy Innocence

The way the whole world changes
Its voice when speaking to a child,
Says a lot about
How sometimes you don't need to be
extraordinarily great
In order to be heard.
Sometimes, you can be your authentic self and
You'd still see people finding excuses
To make your innocence worth it.

Died Alive

Blessed are those
Whose hearts lost all hope,
Whose minds stopped running in loops.
Whose aspirations failed to find meaning
In things that they've deeply wished for.
Whose few plans never got executed
Due to something or the other.
Whose laughter was suppressed by
The weight of their tears,
Whose dreams turned to nightmares,
Whose successes became their setbacks,
Who continued to breathe through their skin but
There was nothing in their air
To keep them alive.

Blessed are those,
Whose hearts were burned in the fires of
Divine plans,
Whose skins retained the marks of all
They'd been through.
Whose souls died before
Their bodies succumbed to death.
Because only their spirit learnt how to live,
Only their spirit learnt it before truly dying!

Blessed are those,
Who died while being alive.

These Words

Who is it
Who can command words to behave properly?
I'm well-assured,
It's not me.
I notice them,
They don't wait for the weekend,
To let me take them to the
museum of blank pages,
They come and ruin my sleep

On weekdays.
Just the moment
After I close my eyes, and
Try to travel to another world.
They tip-toe in,
Teasing me to wake up
In this world, and
Let them have their museum ride.

Ruthless,
Aren't they?
Why can't they come
When I'm seated with a blank page
In front of me?
Full of invisible faith,
That something would definitely strike!

Why can't they come
When I desperately wait for them
With unmovable determination?

Well, I've never, to be honest.
But these white lies seemed promising,
To make a pretty piece,
Like the thousand human promises,
Which make life passable.
Well, I'm not preaching that, and
That was never the point.

All I'm saying is that,
These words find their way to me
Even when I'm not looking for them,
Especially when I'm not looking for them.
These words which disturb my sleep,
Still manage to find warmth
In my mind for them.
These words—selfish and ruthless,
Either take me along with them,
Breaking my patterns,
Or they retreat to their secret place
With the rare possibility of
Being found ever again!

I wonder,
How they still qualify as blessings.
Weird, isn't it?
Or should I say,
They're completely the opposite?

They say blessings are peaceful,
But these words defy that definition to
Be proud of their indiscipline.

They say blessings feel like home,
But these words, if not attended at the right time,
Leave me nowhere,
Neither at home nor anywhere new.

They say blessings don't ruin anything,
But these words ruin my sweet sleep and
My proud punctuality
Just to be heard, just to feel worthy.

I wonder if we were told
Only good things about blessings,
Because, of course, our age-old habit of
Playing this game of duality,
Only instilled the idea that
Good alone makes it work and worth both.
They forgot to include those few
Blessings in disguise!

Making Wishes

Meeting people who
Inspire you to make wishes
You've never made,
But always wished you could,
Is like having an undiscovered gem.
Its worth is unknown to you
Because the people you know
Have never known about it.

The people whose naughtiness
Playfully teaches you that
Possibilities are not as rigid
As rational thoughts in a human mind.
Because possibilities don't know
How real the rationality is
Until you pin them down with your peripheries.

That sheer satisfaction of
Letting those wishes breathe
For the first time in your being,
Is in essence the grandest proof that
There is only a wishful restriction that
Awaits to be freed,
Just to make our world
Look something like a wish-granting factory!

One Story

Oh, our innocent desires to
Find ourselves!
In the blank pages of the books
Before the story starts, or
In between the chapters, and
After the story ends!
Doesn't it already hint so much about
Our inherent self-love?
Or does it rather say,
How in the indecipherable intricacies
We find it easy to call each other dissimilar?
Until we watch that movie,
Listen to that song,
Feel the monochrome in a painting, or
The strokes in a sketch, and
So many things like these,
Which untangles those crisscrosses
To reveal, in their gentlest ways
That at the core, we are all similar,
Or better, we are all one.

Otherwise, why would we
Always try to find an excuse to see ourselves
In the stories of others?

Peculiar Peace

A place on this earth,
Where the pace of the world is at a standstill;
Where the tinkling of windchimes
Still rules over the sound of horns blowing;
Where the photographs on the wall,
Still, bring a wide smile every time.

Where the only chaos is birthed by choice,
Not by unwanted happenings;
Where the only pace allowed is the
One you have chosen,
Not based on popular timelines;
Where the only nostalgia that exists,
Is the one that can make your heart
feel alive again.

Where the windows open to vast spaces,
The verandah still gets good rays of the sun,
The lane has the flashbacks
of a baby's first steps, and
The railings on which the birds still perch.

A place surrounded by
Colourful blooms and greens;
Where the butterflies still visit in numbers.
A place away from big cities;
A place, still rich in its heart.

A place like that, on this earth!
Is it too dreamy? Or is it too absurd?
You might have visited that land already,
Or, you might still do it unknowingly.
I call this place, "my room,"
The one by whom I've been truly fathomed.
But, unlike the version that seemed too dreamy,
There's more to explore in reality.

The place that I've loved,
In the light and the dark.
The door's knob, that I've held
More than any person's hand;
The walls that have seen me breaking,
Like no humans except my mom.
The walls that had
non-judgmentally embraced me,

Like no humans other than my mom.

The nights in there have
witnessed my nightmares;
The days in there have heard my prayers.
The air in those spaces
has answered my questions;
The shadows have taught me
to overcome my fears.
The emptiness of which
has filled me with possibilities;
The companionship that has
made my stories feel heard.
The evenings have seen
a part of me exhausted;
The same evenings have seen
my other part's hunger.
The sounds of thunder as we fell asleep;
The sight of rain pouring incessantly.
The warmth of the tea
in those accompanying evenings;
The chattering of the birds in the early mornings.

A place on the earth where peace is not difficult;
Where peace does not wait for
All the yes and acceptances,
Because it's effortless to find it there.
Rather, where it follows you tip-toed,
In all your delays and disallowances.

Believe me nothing in the world
Can unsettle a person,
Who has found peace
In not knowing things beforehand!
Although, the world never stops wondering or
Trying to inject doubts.
You still stand unshaken in your priorities,
As peace in your progress
is what you have found.

A place on this earth
Where the pace of the world is at a standstill;
Where the tinkling of windchimes
Still rules over the sound of horns blowing;
Where the photographs on the wall
Still bring a wide smile, every time.
It is the place you have consciously created;
It is your home, and
you come back to it every night.